POP BALLADS

Unique, Distinctive Piano Arrangements of 20 Hit Songs

ISBN 978-1-4950-7409-7

T0087279

7777 W. BLUEMOUND RD. P.O. BOX 13819 MILWAUKEE, WI 53213

Visit Hal Leonard Online at
www.halleonard.com

BRIDGE OVER TROUBLE WATER

Words and Music by
PAUL SIMON

FIELDS OF GOLD

Music and Lyrics by
STING

Flowing, moderately

With pedal

AGAINST ALL ODDS
(Take a Look at Me Now)
from AGAINST ALL ODDS

Words and Music by
PHIL COLLINS

Medium Swing

I BELIEVE I CAN FLY

Words and Music by
ROBERT KELLY

HELLO

Words and Music by
LIONEL RICHIE

HOW AM I SUPPOSED TO LIVE WITHOUT YOU

Words and Music by MICHAEL BOLTON
and DOUG JAMES

HOW DEEP IS YOUR LOVE

from the Motion Picture SATURDAY NIGHT FEVER

Words and Music by BARRY GIBB,
ROBIN GIBB and MAURICE GIBB

IN YOUR EYES

Words and Music by
PETER GABRIEL

I WANT TO KNOW WHAT LOVE IS

Words and Music by
MICK JONES

LET IT BE

Words and Music by JOHN LENNON
and PAUL McCARTNEY

Moderately

IMAGINE

Words and Music by
JOHN LENNON

LOOKS LIKE WE MADE IT

Words and Music by RICHARD KERR
and WILL JENNINGS

MORE THAN WORDS

Words and Music by NUNO BETTENCOURT
and GARY CHERONE

RIBBON IN THE SKY

Words and Music by
STEVIE WONDER

Medium Soul Ballad

SHE'S GOT A WAY

Words and Music by
BILLY JOEL

RIGHT HERE WAITING

Words and Music by
RICHARD MARX

TOTAL ECLIPSE OF THE HEART

Words and Music by
JIM STEINMAN

YOU ARE SO BEAUTIFUL

Words and Music by BILLY PRESTON
and BRUCE FISHER

YOU'RE THE INSPIRATION

Words and Music by PETER CETERA
and DAVID FOSTER

Rock Ballad

poco rall.

a tempo
mf

rit.

YOUR SONG

Words and Music by ELTON JOHN
and BERNIE TAUPIN

Moderate Ballad, in 2

With Pedal